Easy Biscuit Cookbook

A Biscuit Book Filled with Delicious Biscuit Recipes and Biscuit Ideas

By
BookSumo Press

Published by
http://www.booksumo.com

ENJOY THE RECIPES?
KEEP ON COOKING
WITH 6 MORE FREE COOKBOOKS!

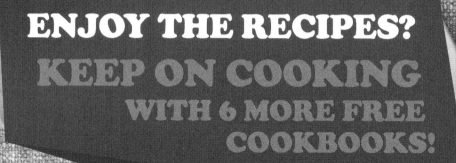

Click the link below and simply enter your email address to join the club and receive your 6 cookbooks.

http://booksumo.com/magnet

https://www.instagram.com/booksumopress/

https://www.facebook.com/booksumo/

LEGAL NOTES

Table of Contents

Pikeville
Biscuits

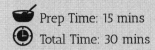 Prep Time: 15 mins

Total Time: 30 mins

Servings per Recipe: 12

Calories	154 kcal
Fat	8 g
Carbohydrates	17.9 g
Protein	2.7 g
Cholesterol	21 mg
Sodium	231 mg

Ingredients

2 C. all-purpose flour
2 1/2 tsp baking powder
1/2 tsp baking soda
1 dash salt
1 tbsp white sugar
1/2 C. butter
3/4 C. buttermilk

Directions

1. Set your oven to 400 degrees F before doing anything else.
2. In a bowl, mix together the flour, baking soda, baking powder, sugar and salt.
3. With a pastry cutter, cut the butter and mix till a coarse crumb forms.
4. Add the buttermilk and mix till well combined.
5. Place the dough onto a floured surface and knead for about 2 minutes.
6. Place the dough onto a baking sheet and roll into a 6x6-inch square, then cut into 12 even sections.
7. Cook in the oven for about 15 minutes.
8. Separate into the biscuits and serve hot.

PARSLEY GARLIC
Cheesy Biscuits

Prep Time: 15 mins
Total Time: 35 mins

Servings per Recipe: 8

Calories	214 kcal
Fat	12.3 g
Carbohydrates	19.9g
Protein	6.4 g
Cholesterol	16 mg
Sodium	732 mg

Ingredients

2 C. biscuit baking mix
1 C. shredded Cheddar cheese
2/3 C. milk
1/2 tsp garlic powder
2 tbsp margarine, melted
2 tsp dried parsley

1 tsp garlic salt

Directions

1. Set your oven to 325 degrees F before doing anything else and grease a cookie sheet.
2. In a large bowl, mix together the baking mix, garlic powder and cheddar cheese.
3. Add the milk and stir to combine.
4. With tablespoon, place the mixture onto prepared cookie sheet in a single layer.
5. Cook in the oven for about 10 minutes.
6. Coat the biscuits with the melted margarine and top with the garlic and parsley.
7. Cook in the oven for about 5 minutes more.

Southern
Chicken Biscuits

🥣 Prep Time: 20 mins
🕐 Total Time: 45 mins

Servings per Recipe: 8
Calories	392 kcal
Fat	20.2 g
Carbohydrates	33.7g
Protein	18.7 g
Cholesterol	41 mg
Sodium	1011 mg

Ingredients

1 tbsp olive oil
6 chicken breast tenderloins
cooking spray
1 (1 lb., 3 oz.) package refrigerated large
flaky layer biscuits
1 (10.75 oz.) can cream of chicken soup
1 1/2 C. frozen mixed vegetables, thawed

1 C. shredded Cheddar cheese, divided

Directions

1. Set your oven to 350 degrees F before doing anything else and grease 16 cups of a muffin tin.
2. In a skillet, heat oil on medium heat and stir fry the chicken for about 10 minutes, flipping once.
3. Remove the chicken from the heat and chop it.
4. Split all the biscuits in half and press the dough halves in each prepared muffin cup, by placing the dough into the bottom and up the sides of each muffin cup.
5. In a bowl, mix together the chicken, mixed vegetables, chicken soup and half of the cheddar cheese.
6. With a tbsp, place the chicken mixture in each cup and sprinkle with the remaining cheese evenly.
7. Cook in the oven for about 14 minutes.

FLUFFY
Biscuits

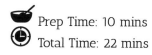 Prep Time: 10 mins

Total Time: 22 mins

Servings per Recipe: 6

Calories	250 kcal
Fat	12.7 g
Carbohydrates	29.9 g
Protein	6.3 g
Cholesterol	33 mg
Sodium	726 mg

Ingredients

2 C. spelt flour
1 tbsp baking powder
1 tsp salt
6 tbsp butter
2/3 C. milk

Directions

1. Set your oven to 450 degrees F before doing anything else.
2. In a large bowl, mix together the flour, baking powder and salt.
3. With a pastry cutter, cut the butter and mix till a coarse crumb forms.
4. Slowly, add the milk and mix till well combined.
5. Place the dough onto floured surface and roll to 1-inch thickness.
6. With a biscuit cutter, cut the dough into biscuits and arrange onto a cookie sheet.
7. Cook in the oven for about 12-15 minutes.

A Biscuit
to Remember

🥣 Prep Time: 20 mins
🕐 Total Time: 40 mins

Servings per Recipe: 9
Calories	235 kcal
Fat	8 g
Carbohydrates	34.9g
Protein	5.4 g
Cholesterol	13 mg
Sodium	632 mg

Ingredients

2 C. self-rising flour
1/8 tsp baking soda
3/4 tsp salt
1 1/2 tbsp white sugar
2 tbsp shortening
2 tbsp butter, softened
1 1/4 C. buttermilk

1 C. all-purpose flour
1 1/2 tbsp butter, melted

Directions

1. Set your oven to 475 degrees F before doing anything else and grease a 10 1/2-inch cast iron skillet.
2. In a bowl, mix together the flour, baking soda, sugar and salt.
3. With a fork, cut the butter and shortening and mix till lumps are pea size.
4. Slowly, add the buttermilk and mix till well combined and keep aside for about 2-3 minutes.
5. Place the dough onto floured surface and roll to 1-inch thickness.
6. In a bowl, place the all-purpose flour.
7. Grease an ice cream scooper with vegetable spray.
8. With the greased scooper, scoop out the dough and place in the flour.
9. With floured hands, pick up each piece and shake off excess flour and shape it into a soft round.
10. Place the biscuits gently into the prepared cast iron skillet and coat the tops with the lightly with melted butter.
11. Cook in the oven for about 16-18 minutes.
12. Cool before serving.

SPICY
Biscuits

Prep Time: 5 mins
Total Time: 20 mins

Servings per Recipe: 6
Calories	397 kcal
Fat	25.2 g
Carbohydrates	36.8g
Protein	5.8 g
Cholesterol	20 mg
Sodium	796 mg

Ingredients

2 1/4 C. self-rising flour
1 C. half-and-half
1/2 C. vegetable oil
1 tbsp Sriracha hot sauce
1 tbsp melted butter
salt to taste

Directions

1. Set your oven to 425 degrees F before doing anything else.
2. In a bowl, mix together the flour, oil, half-and-half and hot sauce and mix till a lumpy dough forms.
3. Roll the dough into 2-inch balls and place on a baking sheet.
4. Cook in the oven for about 15 minutes.
5. Coat with the melted butter and serve with a sprinkling of the salt.

British
Biscuits

🥣 Prep Time: 10 mins
🕐 Total Time: 20 mins

Servings per Recipe: 48
Calories	223 kcal
Fat	7.9 g
Carbohydrates	37.7g
Protein	1.2 g
Cholesterol	21 mg
Sodium	56 mg

Ingredients

2 C. butter, softened
1 C. white sugar
4 C. sifted all-purpose flour
1 C. raspberry preserves
24 maraschino cherries
8 C. confectioners' sugar
1/2 C. milk

Directions

1. Set your oven to 350 degrees F before doing anything else.
2. In a large bowl, add the sugar and butter and beat till smooth.
3. Slowly, add the flour and mix till well combined.
4. Place the dough onto floured surface and roll to 14-inch thickness.
5. With a cookie cutter, cut into round biscuits and arrange onto a cookie sheet.
6. Cook in the oven for about 8-10 minutes.
7. Spread 1 tsp of the jam between the 2 cookies to make a sandwich.
8. Repeat with the remaining cookies.
9. In a medium bowl, add the confectioners' sugar and slowly, add the milk and mix till the icing changes into a spreadable consistency.
10. Spread the icing on top of the sandwiched cookies and place a cherry on top.

ITALIAN
Biscuits

Prep Time: 20 mins
Total Time: 20 mins

Servings per Recipe: 8

Calories	472 kcal
Fat	29.6 g
Carbohydrates	42.3g
Protein	6.7 g
Cholesterol	70 mg
Sodium	77 mg

Ingredients

1/2 C. chopped blanched almonds
5 oz. amarettini cookies, crumbled into
1/2 inch pieces
3 tbsp dark rum
3/4 C. semisweet chocolate chips
1 C. heavy cream, chilled

3 tbsp brandy
1 quart vanilla ice cream, softened

Directions

1. Set your oven to 350 degrees F before doing anything else.
2. Arrange the almonds on a baking dish and cook in the oven for about 5-8 minutes.
3. Remove from the oven and keep aside to cool completely.
4. In a bowl, add the crumbled cookies, rum, chocolate chips and almonds and toss to coat well.
5. In a large bowl, add the cream and beat till thickened.
6. Add the brandy and beat till the soft peaks form.
7. Place the whipped cream over the cookie mixture.
8. In whipped cream bowl, now beat ice cream just till softened.
9. Fold cookie and cream mixture into ice cream and freeze till serving.

Healthy
Biscuits

🥣 Prep Time: 15 mins
🕐 Total Time: 30 mins

Servings per Recipe: 12

Calories	57 kcal
Fat	5.5 g
Carbohydrates	1.5g
Protein	1.1 g
Cholesterol	31 mg
Sodium	227 mg

Ingredients

2 1/2 C. blanched almond flour
1 tsp baking soda
3/4 tsp sea salt
1/4 C. coconut oil, melted and cooled
2 large eggs at room temperature, beaten
1 tbsp raw honey

Directions

1. Set your oven to 350 degrees F before doing anything else and line a baking sheet with parchment paper.
2. In a bowl, mix together the flour, baking soda and salt.
3. Add the coconut oil and stir till fluffy.
4. Add the honey and eggs and mix till dough ball forms.
5. With an ice cream scooper, place the dough onto prepared cookie sheet and with your fingers, press to make a biscuit.
6. Cook in the oven for about 15 minutes.

AROMATIC
Biscuits

Prep Time: 15 mins
Total Time: 30 mins

Servings per Recipe: 10
Calories	163 kcal
Fat	10.7 g
Carbohydrates	14.7g
Protein	2.3 g
Cholesterol	16 mg
Sodium	396 mg

Ingredients

1/3 C. butter
1 tsp prepared Dijon-style mustard
1 tbsp chopped fresh rosemary
2 tbsp chopped fresh basil leaves
2 drops hot pepper sauce
1 (12 oz.) package refrigerated biscuit

dough

Directions

1. Set your oven to 400 degrees F before doing anything else and lightly, grease a cookie sheet.
2. In a pan, melt the butter on medium heat.
3. Add the Dijon mustard, hot pepper sauce and fresh herbs and stir to combine.
4. Coat the biscuit dough pieces in the butter mixture and place onto the prepared cookie sheet.
5. Cook in the oven for about 15-20 minutes.

Southern
Biscuits

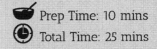 Prep Time: 10 mins

Total Time: 25 mins

Servings per Recipe: 8
Calories	336 kcal
Fat	11.6 g
Carbohydrates	49 g
Protein	8 g
Cholesterol	17 mg
Sodium	939 mg

Ingredients

4 C. self-rising flour
1 pinch salt
3 tbsp room-temperature vegetable shortening
1 3/4 C. buttermilk
1/4 C. melted butter for brushing

Directions

1. Set your oven to 475 degrees F before doing anything else and grease an 8-inch cake pan.
2. In a large bowl, sift together the flour and salt.
3. Make a well in the center of the flour mixture.
4. Add the splash of the buttermilk and 2 walnut-size lumps of the shortening in the center and mix till well combined.
5. Add the buttermilk about 1/4 C. of at a time, mixing till a sticky dough forms.
6. Roll the dough into 8 large balls and place into the prepared cake pan, working around the outside and putting the last one in middle to fill the pan.
7. With the back of the fingers, press the dough balls to flatten until into 3/4-1-inch thickness.
8. Cook in the oven for about 15-20 minutes.
9. Coat the top of the biscuits with the melted butter.

ZINGY
Biscuits

Prep Time: 20 mins
Total Time: 35 mins

Servings per Recipe: 12
Calories   169 kcal
Fat   10.1 g
Carbohydrates   17.1g
Protein   2.8 g
Cholesterol   27 mg
Sodium   376 mg

Ingredients

3/4 C. milk
1 tbsp fresh lime juice
2 C. all-purpose flour
1 tbsp baking powder
1 lime, zested
1 tsp salt

1/2 tsp baking soda
10 tbsp unsalted butter, cut into pieces

Directions

1. Set your oven to 400 degrees F before doing anything else.
2. In a bowl, mix together the milk and lime juice.
3. In another bowl, mix together the flour, baking soda, baking powder, lime zest and salt.
4. With a pastry cutter, cut the butter and mix till a coarse crumb forms.
5. Add the milk mixture into the flour mixture and mix till well combined.
6. Place the dough onto a lightly floured smooth surface and knead a few times.
7. Gently shape the dough into a 3/4-inch thick disk and with a 2 1/2-inch floured cutter, cut into 12 biscuits.
8. Place the biscuits onto a baking sheet.
9. Cook in the oven for about 15-20 minutes.

Traditional
Scottish Biscuits

Prep Time: 30 mins

Total Time: 40 mins

Servings per Recipe: 18	
Calories	322 kcal
Fat	11.1 g
Carbohydrates	54.5g
Protein	2.5 g
Cholesterol	48 mg
Sodium	155 mg

Ingredients

1/2 C. butter, softened
1/2 C. white sugar
2 eggs
2 C. all-purpose flour
1 tbsp baking powder
1 tbsp allspice
1 tbsp ground cinnamon

1/2 C. butter, softened
1/8 tsp salt
3 C. sifted confectioners' sugar
1/4 C. milk, or as needed
1 1/2 tsp vanilla extract
1 C. strawberry jam
1 (10 oz.) jar maraschino cherries, drained

Directions

1. Set your oven to 350 degrees F before doing anything else.
2. In a large bowl add the 1/2 C. of the butter and white sugar and beat till smooth.
3. Add the eggs one a time, mixing till well combine.
4. In another bowl, mix together the flour, baking powder, allspice and cinnamon.
5. Add the flour mixture into the butter mixture and mix till a stiff dough forms.
6. Place the dough onto a lightly floured surface and roll into 1/8-1/4-inch thickness.
7. With a biscuit cutter, cut into circles and place onto ungreased baking sheets about 2 inches apart.
8. Cook in the oven for about 10 minutes.
9. Cool cookies on wire racks for at least 15 minutes.
10. Meanwhile for the frosting in a small bowl, add the butter and salt and beat till soft.
11. Slowly, add the confectioners' sugar and vanilla until and mix till smooth and light.
12. Spread the strawberry jam over the one side of a cookie and top with another cookie to make a jam sandwich.
13. Spread frosting on top and place a maraschino cherry half in the center.
14. Repeat with the remaining cookies.

ARROWROOT
Biscuits

Prep Time: 50 mins
Total Time: 1 hr

Servings per Recipe: 18

Calories	86 kcal
Fat	2.9 g
Carbohydrates	14.1g
Protein	1.1 g
Cholesterol	17 mg
Sodium	68 mg

Ingredients

1/4 C. butter, softened
1/2 C. white sugar
1 egg
1/2 tsp vanilla extract
1 C. all-purpose flour
1/2 C. arrowroot flour

1/2 tsp baking powder
1/4 tsp salt

Directions

1. Set your oven to 350 degrees F before doing anything else and line the cookie sheets with the parchment papers.
2. In a bowl, add the butter and sugar and beat till just smooth.
3. Add the egg and vanilla and beat well.
4. In another bowl, mix together the flour, arrowroot flour, baking powder and salt.
5. Add the flour mixture into the butter mixture and mix well.
6. Divide dough in 2 portions.
7. On a lightly floured surface, roll both the dough portions separately into 1/8-inch thickness and cut into 2 1/2-inch rounds.
8. Place the rounds onto the prepared cookie sheets and with a fork, prick them.
9. Cook in the oven for about 8-10 minutes.

Australian
Biscuits

Prep Time: 15 mins
Total Time: 30 mins

Servings per Recipe: 22
Calories	90 kcal
Fat	5.1 g
Carbohydrates	10.6g
Protein	0.8 g
Cholesterol	11 mg
Sodium	49 mg

Ingredients

3/4 C. rolled oats
3/4 C. sweetened flaked coconut
1/2 C. all-purpose flour
1/2 C. white sugar
1/2 tsp baking powder
2 tbsp boiling water
1/2 C. butter, melted

1 tbsp golden syrup

Directions

1. Set your oven to 350 degrees F before doing anything else and lightly, grease the cookie sheets.
2. In a bowl, mix together the flour, oats, coconut and sugar.
3. In another bowl, dissolve the baking powder in the boiling water.
4. Add the butter and golden syrup and mix well.
5. Add the butter mixture into the oat mixture and mix till a dough forms.
6. With a tbsp, place the dough onto the prepared cookie sheets about 2 inches apart and with a lightly floured fork, flatten the biscuits.
7. Cook in the oven for about 15 minutes.

GOOEY
Arrowroot Biscuits

Prep Time: 15 mins
Total Time: 30 mins

Servings per Recipe: 8
Calories	560 kcal
Fat	27.7 g
Carbohydrates	86.3g
Protein	8.7 g
Cholesterol	19 mg
Sodium	609 mg

Ingredients

1 1/4 C. Reduced Fat Bisquick(R)
1 C. whole wheat baking mix
2/3 C. buttermilk
2 C. HERSHEY(R)'S Cinnamon Chips
1 C. cinnamon coated raisins
3 tbsp melted butter

1/2 C. confectioners' sugar
1 tbsp melted butter
1 tbsp water

Directions

1. Set your oven to 425 degrees F before doing anything else.
2. In a food processor, add the cinnamon chips and pulse till grounded roughly.
3. Transfer 1/2 of the chips into a bowl.
4. Continue to pulse the remaining chips till ground finely.
5. In a large bowl, mix together the baking mixes, 1 C. of the roughly grounded cinnamon chips and raisins.
6. Make a well in the center of the mixture and add the buttermilk, and stir till the dough comes together.
7. Place the dough onto a lightly floured smooth surface and knead gently for about 1 minute.
8. Flatten the dough to an 8x10-inch rectangle and coat with the melted butter.
9. Sprinkle with the finely ground cinnamon chips evenly.
10. Starting from one long side, roll up the dough and pinch seams and ends to seal.
11. Cut the roll crosswise into 8 equal slices and place in a 13x9-inch ungreased baking dish.
12. Cook in the oven for about 12 minutes.
13. In a bowl, add the confectioners' sugar, 1 tbsp of the melted butter and water and mix till smooth.
14. Drizzle glaze over the hot biscuits.

Old-Fashioned
Biscuits

🥣 Prep Time: 10 mins

🕐 Total Time: 20 mins

Servings per Recipe: 12
Calories	114 kcal
Fat	4.1 g
Carbohydrates	16.6 g
Protein	2.4 g
Cholesterol	2 mg
Sodium	398 mg

Ingredients

2 1/2 C. buttermilk baking mix
1 tsp baking powder
1 pinch salt
2/3 C. milk
1/2 tbsp malt vinegar

Directions

1. Set your oven to 450 degrees F before doing anything else and lightly, grease 2 cookie sheets.
2. In a large bowl, mix together the baking mix, baking powder and salt.
3. Add the milk and vinegar and mix till a loose dough forms.
4. Place the dough onto a lightly floured surface and knead for about 10 times.
5. Divide the dough into 12 equal pieces and place on prepared baking sheets.
6. Cook in the oven for about 8-10 minutes.

AMERICAN
Biscuits

Prep Time: 25 mins
Total Time: 40 mins

Servings per Recipe: 24
Calories	67 kcal
Fat	2.9 g
Carbohydrates	8.9g
Protein	1.2 g
Cholesterol	4 mg
Sodium	31 mg

Ingredients

2 C. all-purpose flour
1/4 tsp salt
1/4 tsp baking powder
1 1/2 tbsp white sugar
1/4 C. butter
1/3 C. light cream

2 tbsp cold water

Directions

1. Set your oven to 450 degrees F before doing anything else and lightly, grease the cookie sheets.
2. In a bowl, sift together the flour, baking powder, sugar and salt.
3. With a fork cut the butter into the flour mixture and mix till a coarse meal forms.
4. Slowly add the cream and with a wooden spoon, mix till the dough forms into a ball. (Add water if needed.)
5. Place the dough onto a smooth surface and knead slightly.
6. With a rolling pin, roll the dough a few times to form it into a rough rectangle.
7. Fold the dough over, and then roll it again and repeat this process for about 15 minutes.
8. Roll the dough into 1/4-inch thickness and cut into 2-inch rounds.
9. With a fork, prick the top a few times and place onto the prepared cookie sheets.
10. Cook in the oven for about 15 minutes.

Simple
Buttermilk Biscuits

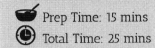 Prep Time: 15 mins

Total Time: 25 mins

Servings per Recipe: 12

Calories	147 kcal
Fat	8 g
Carbohydrates	16.1g
Protein	2.6 g
Cholesterol	21 mg
Sodium	333 mg

Ingredients

2 C. self-rising flour
1/2 C. butter
2/3 C. buttermilk

Directions

1. Set your oven to 450 degrees F before doing anything else and lightly, grease a cookie sheet.
2. In a large bowl, add the flour and with a pastry cutter, cut the butter and mix till a coarse crumb forms.
3. Slowly, add the buttermilk and mix till well combined.
4. With a round tbsp, place the mixture onto the prepared cookie sheet.
5. Cook in the oven for about 10 minutes.

TRADITIONAL
English Biscuits

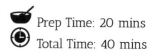 Prep Time: 20 mins

Total Time: 40 mins

Servings per Recipe: 24

Calories	73 kcal
Fat	4.1 g
Carbohydrates	8.2g
Protein	0.8 g
Cholesterol	19 mg
Sodium	118 mg

Ingredients

1/2 C. butter, softened
3/8 C. white sugar
1 tsp vanilla extract
1 egg yolk
1 C. self-rising flour
2 tbsp cornstarch

1/4 tsp salt
1/4 C. rolled oats

Directions

1. Set your oven to 375 degrees F before doing anything else and lightly, grease the cookie sheets.
2. In a bowl, add the butter and sugar and beat till light and fluffy.
3. Add the egg yolk and vanilla extract and beat well.
4. In another bowl, sift together the flour, cornstarch and salt.
5. Add the flour mixture into the butter mixture and mix till a dough forms.
6. Make about 1/2-inch 20-24 small balls and roll each ball in the oats.
7. Arrange onto the prepared cookie sheets about 2 inches apart.
8. Cook in the oven for about 15-20 minutes.

Caraway
Lemon Biscuits

Prep Time: 50 mins
Total Time: 1 hr

Servings per Recipe: 12
Calories	558 kcal
Fat	27.7 g
Carbohydrates	70g
Protein	8 g
Cholesterol	47 mg
Sodium	81 mg

Ingredients

5 1/2 C. all-purpose flour
1 1/2 tsp lemon zest
1 1/2 C. white sugar
1 1/2 tsp baking powder
1 1/2 C. shortening
3 eggs
3 tbsp milk

3 tbsp caraway seed

Directions

1. Set your oven to 375 degrees F before doing anything else and line the cookie sheets with the parchment papers.
2. In a large bowl, mix together the flour, baking powder and sugar.
3. With a pastry cutter, cut the butter and mix till a coarse crumb forms.
4. In another bowl, add the eggs, milk, seeds and lemon zest and beat well.
5. Add the milk mixture into the flour mixture and mix till smooth.
6. Place the dough onto floured surface and roll to 1/4-inch thickness.
7. With a 2-inch round biscuit cutter, cut the dough into biscuits and arrange onto the prepared cookie sheets.
8. Cook in the oven for about 7-10 minutes.

HONEY CARDAMOM
Biscuits

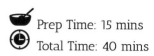 Prep Time: 15 mins

Total Time: 40 mins

Servings per Recipe: 6

Calories	286 kcal
Fat	7.7 g
Carbohydrates	47.9 g
Protein	7.4 g
Cholesterol	3 mg
Sodium	272 mg

Ingredients

1 1/2 C. all-purpose flour
1/2 C. nonfat dry milk powder
2 tsp baking powder
1 tsp ground cardamom
1/8 tsp salt
1/3 C. warm milk

1/3 C. honey
3 tbsp canola oil
1/2 tsp vanilla extract
1 tbsp turbinado sugar

Directions

1. Set your oven to 425 degrees F before doing anything else and lightly, grease a cookie sheet.
2. In a bowl, mix together the flour, dry milk powder, baking powder, cardamom and salt.
3. In another bowl, mix together the warm milk, honey, oil, and vanilla extract.
4. Add the milk mixture into the flour mixture and mix till a dough forms.
5. Place the dough onto a floured surface and gently pat into a 9x3-inch rectangle.
6. With a sharp knife, cut the dough into 3 (3-inch) squares.
7. Cut each square on the diagonal to make 6 triangles, and arrange the triangles onto the prepared cookie sheet.
8. Cook in the oven for about 6 minutes.
9. Remove from the oven and sprinkle the tops of the biscuits with the turbinado sugar.
10. Cook in the oven for about 8 minutes more.

Sourdough
Biscuits

Prep Time: 15 mins
Total Time: 2 hr

Servings per Recipe: 12
Calories	79 kcal
Fat	4.7 g
Carbohydrates	8.2g
Protein	1.1 g
Cholesterol	0 mg
Sodium	156 mg

Ingredients

1 C. Herman Sourdough Starter
1 C. all-purpose flour
1/4 tsp baking soda
2 tsp baking powder
1/4 tsp salt
1/4 C. vegetable oil

Directions

1. Lightly, grease a cookie sheet.
2. Bring Herman Starter to room temperature.
3. Stir together flour, baking soda, baking soda and salt.
4. Add the flour mixture and oil into Herman Starter and stir till a soft dough forms.
5. Place the dough onto a lightly floured surface and knead till smooth.
6. Roll the dough and with a biscuit cutter, cut the biscuits.
7. Place the biscuits onto the prepared cookie sheet.
8. Cover the cookie sheet and keep aside in the warm place for about 1 hour.
9. Set your oven to 350 degrees F.
10. Cook in the oven for about 30 minutes.

CORNMEAL TEA
Biscuits

🥣 Prep Time: 15 mins

🕐 Total Time: 1 hr 20 mins

Servings per Recipe: 10

Calories	196 kcal
Fat	3.9 g
Carbohydrates	33.7g
Protein	6 g
Cholesterol	1 mg
Sodium	475 mg

Ingredients

1 1/2 tsp active dry yeast
1 tsp white sugar
1 C. warm water
3 C. unbleached flour
2 tsp salt
3/4 C. milk

2 tbsp vegetable oil
1/4 C. cornmeal

Directions

1. In a small bowl, dissolve the sugar and yeast in warm water and keep aside for about 10 minutes.
2. To make crumpet rings, cut the aluminum foil into 7x12-inch pieces.
3. Fold in half lengthwise and then in thirds, making 6 layers.
4. Form into a 3 1/2-inch diameter circle and tape shut on the outside.
5. In a large bowl, mix together the flour and salt.
6. Add the milk, oil and yeast mixture and beat well till smooth.
7. Cover with plastic wrap and keep in a warm place for about 60 minutes.
8. Lightly grease the inside of the crumpet rings and then, dip the rings in cornmeal.
9. Heat a frying pan on medium-low heat and sprinkle with the cornmeal.
10. Place the rings on the frying pan and deflate the mixture by stirring.
11. Place 1/4 C. of the mixture into each ring and cook slowly for about 10 minutes.
12. Carefully remove the rings and flip the biscuits and cook for about 8 minutes.

Biscuits
for Autumn

Prep Time: 30 mins
Total Time: 50 mins

Servings per Recipe: 36
Calories	62 kcal
Fat	2.7 g
Carbohydrates	8.5g
Protein	1 g
Cholesterol	7 mg
Sodium	92 mg

Ingredients

2 1/2 C. all-purpose flour
3 tbsp packed brown sugar
1 tbsp baking powder
1/2 tsp salt
1/4 tsp ground nutmeg
1/4 tsp ground cinnamon
1/4 tsp ground ginger

1/2 C. butter, sliced
2 C. pumpkin puree

Directions

1. Set your oven to 400 degrees F before doing anything else and grease a large cookie sheet.
2. In a large bowl, mix together the flour, baking powder, brown sugar and spices.
3. With a pastry cutter, cut the butter and mix till a coarse crumb forms.
4. Add the pumpkin puree and mix till a soft dough forms.
5. Place the dough onto floured surface and roll to 1/2-inch thickness.
6. With a biscuit cutter, cut the dough into 2-inch round biscuits and arrange onto a cookie sheet.
7. Cook in the oven for about 15-20 minutes.

CLASSIC
Cheddar Cheese Chive Biscuits

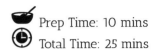 Prep Time: 10 mins

Total Time: 25 mins

Servings per Recipe: 8
Calories	356 kcal
Fat	23.4 g
Carbohydrates	30.6 g
Protein	6.6 g
Cholesterol	39 mg
Sodium	1278 mg

Ingredients

2 (10 oz.) cans refrigerated biscuit
dough
1/2 C. shredded Cheddar cheese
1/2 C. butter, melted
2 tsp garlic salt
1 tbsp chopped fresh chives

Directions

1. Set your oven to 375 degrees F before doing anything else.
2. Unwrap each the tube of biscuit dough and place the two logs onto a baking sheet in the same pattern they were in the can.
3. Gently separate biscuits, keeping them still attached on the bottom and sprinkle the cheddar cheese between each biscuit.
4. In a small bowl, mix together the melted butter and garlic salt.
5. Coat each biscuit log with the butter mixture evenly and top with the chives.
6. Cook in the oven for about 12-15 minutes.

Homemade Honey
Molasses Biscuits

🥘 Prep Time: 10 mins

🕐 Total Time: 25 mins

Servings per Recipe: 12

Calories	65 kcal
Fat	0.7 g
Carbohydrates	12.1g
Protein	2.2 g
Cholesterol	16 mg
Sodium	13 mg

Ingredients

1 egg, beaten
2 tbsp honey
2 tbsp molasses
2 tbsp vanilla extract
3/4 C. whole wheat flour
1 1/2 tbsp non-fat dry milk
1 tbsp soy flour

1 tbsp wheat germ

Directions

1. Set your oven to 350 degrees F before doing anything else.
2. In a medium bowl, add the egg, honey, molasses and vanilla and mix till well combined.
3. In another bowl, mix together the whole-wheat flour, soy flour, dry milk and wheat germ.
4. Add the flour mixture into the molasses mixture and mix till a smooth dough forms.
5. Place the dough onto a lightly floured surface and roll to 1/4-inch thickness.
6. Cut in to finger length strips and arrange onto an ungreased cookie sheet.
7. Cook in the oven for about 15 minutes.

LIGHT
Biscuits

Prep Time: 20 mins
Total Time: 40 mins

Servings per Recipe: 20

Calories	96 kcal
Fat	5.4 g
Carbohydrates	10.2g
Protein	1.6 g
Cholesterol	1 mg
Sodium	218 mg

Ingredients

2 C. all-purpose flour
4 tsp baking powder
1 tsp salt
1/2 C. shortening
3/4 C. milk

Directions

1. Set your oven to 400 degrees F before doing anything else and lightly, grease a cookie sheet.
2. In a large bowl, mix together the flour, baking powder and salt.
3. With a pastry cutter, cut the shortening and mix till a coarse crumb forms.
4. Slowly, add the milk and mix till well combined.
5. Place the dough onto floured surface and roll to 1/2-inch thickness.
6. With a biscuit cutter, cut the dough into biscuits and arrange onto a cookie sheet, then keep aside for a few minutes.
7. Cook in the oven for about 12-15 minutes.

2nd Grade
Cocoa Biscuits

🥄 Prep Time: 20 mins
🕐 Total Time: 50 mins

Servings per Recipe: 6
Calories	255 kcal
Fat	7.3 g
Carbohydrates	41.2g
Protein	6.8 g
Cholesterol	73 mg
Sodium	212 mg

Ingredients

1/3 C. instant hot cocoa mix
1/3 C. white sugar
2 eggs
1 1/2 tsp baking powder
1 C. rolled oats
1 C. all-purpose flour
1/3 C. milk

2 tbsp butter

Directions

1. Set your oven to 350 degrees F before doing anything else and lightly, grease a cookie sheet.
2. In a bowl, mix together the flour, oats, powdered hot chocolate, sugar and baking powder.
3. Add the butter and mix well.
4. In another bowl, add the eggs and milk and beat well.
5. Add the egg mixture into the flour mixture and mix till well combined.
6. With the tbsp, place the dough onto the prepared baking sheet and keep aside for about 5 minutes.
7. Cook in the oven for about 10-15 minutes.

BUTTERMILK
Bacon Biscuits

Prep Time: 10 mins
Total Time: 20 mins

Servings per Recipe: 10
Calories	482 kcal
Fat	39.7 g
Carbohydrates	13.3g
Protein	17.6 g
Cholesterol	164 mg
Sodium	896 mg

Ingredients

1 (10 oz.) can refrigerated buttermilk
biscuit dough
1 lb. turkey bacon
5 eggs
1/4 C. milk
3 tbsp butter, softened

10 slices Cheddar cheese

Directions

1. Set your oven to 400 degrees F before doing anything else.
2. Arrange the biscuits on an ungreased cookie sheet about 2 inches apart and cook in the oven for about 8-11 minutes.
3. Heat a large skillet on medium-high heat and cook the bacon till browned completely.
4. Drain the excess grease from the skillet.
5. In a large bowl, add the eggs and milk and beat well.
6. Heat a lightly greased skillet on medium heat and scramble eggs to your desired doneness.
7. Cut open the biscuits and lightly butter them.
8. Layer with the eggs, bacon and cheese.

British Rolled Oat Biscuits

Prep Time: 15 mins
Total Time: 20 mins

Servings per Recipe: 12
Calories   90 kcal
Fat   4.1 g
Carbohydrates   12.4g
Protein   1.6 g
Cholesterol   11 mg
Sodium   51 mg

Ingredients

3/4 C. whole wheat flour
1/4 C. all-purpose flour
1/2 tsp baking powder
1 tbsp rolled oats
4 tbsp butter
4 tbsp brown sugar
4 tbsp milk

Directions

1. Set your oven to 375 degrees F before doing anything else and grease the cookie sheet.
2. In a large bowl, sift together the flour and baking powder.
3. Add the oatmeal and mix well.
4. In another bowl, add the butter and sugar and beat till creamy.
5. Add the butter mixture into the flour mixture and mix till a thick paste forms.
6. Place the dough onto a floured surface and knead till smooth.
7. Roll out the dough to 1/8-inch thickness and with a cookie cutter, cut into the rounds about 2 1/2 inches in diameter.
8. Place the biscuits onto the prepared cookie sheets and with a fork, prick them.
9. Cook in the oven for about 15-18 minutes.

5-INGREDIENT
Biscuits

Prep Time: 15 mins
Total Time: 25 mins

Servings per Recipe: 10
Calories	191 kcal
Fat	10.9 g
Carbohydrates	20.2g
Protein	3.2 g
Cholesterol	1 mg
Sodium	225 mg

Ingredients

2 C. all-purpose flour
1 tbsp baking powder
1/2 tsp salt
1/2 C. shortening
3/4 C. milk

Directions

1. Set your oven to 450 degrees F before doing anything else.
2. In a large bowl sift together the flour, baking powder and salt.
3. With a pastry cutter, cut the shortening and mix till a coarse crumb forms.
4. Slowly, add the milk and mix till well combined.
5. Place the dough onto floured surface and roll to 1/2-inch thickness.
6. With a biscuit cutter, cut the dough into biscuits and arrange onto a cookie sheet.
7. Cook in the oven for about 10 minutes.

Mayo'lina
Biscuits

🥣 Prep Time: 10 mins

🕐 Total Time: 22 mins

Servings per Recipe: 12

Calories	133 kcal
Fat	6.1 g
Carbohydrates	16.6g
Protein	2.8 g
Cholesterol	4 mg
Sodium	312 mg

Ingredients

2 C. self-rising flour
1 C. milk
6 tbsp mayonnaise

Directions

1. Set your oven to 400 degrees F before doing anything else and grease a cookie sheet.
2. In a large bowl, mix together the flour, milk and mayonnaise and mix till well combined.
3. With a tbsp, place the dough onto the prepared cookie sheets.
4. Cook in the oven for about 12 minutes.

HOMEMADE
Biscuit Mixture

Prep Time: 20 mins
Total Time: 40 mins

Servings per Recipe: 24
Calories	351 kcal
Fat	17.6 g
Carbohydrates	43.1g
Protein	5.4 g
Cholesterol	0 mg
Sodium	682 mg

Ingredients

10 C. all-purpose flour
1/2 C. baking powder
1/4 C. white sugar
2 tsp salt
2 C. shortening

Directions

1. In a large bowl mix together the flour, sugar, baking powder and salt.
2. With a pastry cutter, cut the shortening and mix till a coarse crumb forms.
3. Store in an airtight container for up to 6 weeks.

Biscuit
Pot Pie

🥣 Prep Time: 30 mins
🕐 Total Time: 1 hr

Servings per Recipe: 6
Calories	577 kcal
Fat	31.2 g
Carbohydrates	44.7g
Protein	27.1 g
Cholesterol	120 mg
Sodium	1000 mg

Ingredients

1/4 C. butter
1 small onion, chopped
3 celery ribs, chopped
3 carrots, chopped
2/3 C. frozen peas
3 tbsp chopped fresh parsley
1/4 tsp dried thyme
1/4 C. all-purpose flour

2 C. lower-sodium chicken broth
2/3 C. half-and-half cream
salt and ground black pepper to taste
3 C. cooked chicken, cut into bite-size pieces
1 (16.3 oz.) can refrigerated flaky-style biscuits
1 egg yolk, beaten
1 tbsp water

Directions

1. Set your oven to 350 degrees F before doing anything else.
2. In a large skillet, melt the butter on medium-low heat and sauté the onion, carrot and celery for about 15 minutes.
3. Stir in the flour, peas and herbs and cook, stirring continuously for about 5 minutes.
4. Slowly, add the chicken broth and half-and-half, beating continuously and cook until the sauce becomes thick.
5. Season with the salt and black pepper and stir in the chicken meat.
6. Transfer the chicken mixture into a large baking dish and place the biscuits on top of the filling.
7. In a small bowl, add the egg yolk and water and beat well.
8. Coat the top of the biscuits with the egg yolk mixture.
9. Cook in the oven for about 20-25 minutes.

TARTAR
Biscuits

Prep Time: 10 mins
Total Time: 20 mins

Servings per Recipe: 4
Calories   465 kcal
Fat   24.5 g
Carbohydrates   53.1g
Protein   8.2 g
Cholesterol   65 mg
Sodium   834 mg

Ingredients

2 C. all-purpose flour
1/2 tsp salt
4 tsp baking powder
1/2 tsp cream of tartar
2 tsp white sugar
1/2 C. butter, chilled and diced

3/4 C. milk

Directions

1. Set your oven to 450 degrees F before doing anything else.
2. In a large bowl, mix together the flour, sugar, baking powder, cream of tartar and salt.
3. With a pastry cutter, cut the butter and mix till a coarse crumb forms.
4. Make a well in the center and slowly, add the milk and mix till well combined.
5. Place the dough onto floured surface and roll to 3/4-inch thickness.
6. Cut the dough into 2-inch round biscuits and arrange onto a cookie sheet.
7. Cook in the oven for about 10 minutes.

30-Minute
Drop Biscuits

Prep Time: 15 mins
Total Time: 30 mins

Servings per Recipe: 12
Calories	157 kcal
Fat	8.3 g
Carbohydrates	17.8g
Protein	2.9 g
Cholesterol	22 mg
Sodium	196 mg

Ingredients

2 C. all-purpose flour
1 tbsp baking powder
2 tsp white sugar
1/2 tsp cream of tartar
1/4 tsp salt
1/2 C. melted butter
1 C. milk

Directions

1. Set your oven to 450 degrees F before doing anything else and lightly, grease a cookie sheet.
2. In a large bowl, mix together the flour, sugar, baking powder, cream of tartar and salt.
3. Add the butter and milk and mix till well combined.
4. With a tbsp arrange the dough onto a cookie sheet.
5. Cook in the oven for about 8-12 minutes.

BANANA
Peanut Butter Biscuits

Prep Time: 25 mins
Total Time: 55 mins

Servings per Recipe: 4

Calories	465 kcal
Fat	24.5 g
Carbohydrates	53.1g
Protein	8.2 g
Cholesterol	65 mg
Sodium	834 mg

Ingredients

1 egg
1/3 C. peanut butter
1/2 C. mashed banana
1 tbsp honey
1 C. whole wheat flour
1/2 C. wheat germ

1 egg white, lightly beaten, for brushing

Directions

1. Set your oven to 300 degrees F before doing anything else and grease a cookie sheet.
2. In a bowl, add the egg, peanut butter, banana and honey and mix till well combined.
3. Stir in the flour and wheat germ and mix well.
4. Place the dough out onto a floured surface and roll to 1/4-inch thickness.
5. With a cookie cutter, cut the dough into desired shapes and place onto prepared baking sheet.
6. Coat the tops of the biscuits with the egg white and cook in the oven for about 30 minutes.

Southern
Biscuits with Gravy

Prep Time: 5 mins
Total Time: 15 mins

Servings per Recipe: 8
Calories	333 kcal
Fat	18.7 g
Carbohydrates	30.8g
Protein	9.8 g
Cholesterol	25 mg
Sodium	767 mg

Ingredients

1 (16 oz.) can refrigerated jumbo
buttermilk biscuits
1 (9.6 oz.) package Jimmy Dean(R) Original
Hearty beef Sausage Crumbles
1/4 C. flour
2 1/2 C. milk
Salt and ground black pepper to taste

Directions

1. Cook the biscuits in the oven according to package's directions.
2. Meanwhile heat a large skillet on medium heat and cook the sausage for about 5-6 minutes.
3. Drain the excess grease from the skillet.
4. Stir in the flour and slowly, add the milk.
5. Boil the mixture till thickens, stirring continuously.
6. Reduce the heat to medium-low and simmer for about 2 minutes, stirring continuously.
7. Stir in the salt and pepper.
8. Split the biscuits in half and place 2 halves on each of 8 plates.
9. Top with about 1/3 C. of the gravy.

CALIFORNIA
Cheese Biscuits

Prep Time: 20 mins
Total Time: 40 mins

Servings per Recipe: 20
Calories	139 kcal
Fat	6.3 g
Carbohydrates	17.5g
Protein	3.2 g
Cholesterol	17 mg
Sodium	550 mg

Ingredients

4 C. baking mix
3 oz. Cheddar cheese, shredded
1 1/3 C. water
1/2 C. melted butter
1 tsp garlic powder
1/4 tsp salt

1/8 tsp onion powder
1/8 tsp dried parsley

Directions

1. Set your oven to 375 degrees F before doing anything else and line a cookie sheet with a parchment paper.
2. In a bowl, add the baking mix, cheese and water and mix till a firm dough forms.
3. With a small scoop, place dough on the prepared cookie sheet.
4. Cook in the oven for about 10-12 minutes.
5. In a bowl, mix together the melted butter, parsley, garlic powder, onion powder and salt.
6. Remove from the oven and immediately, coat the baked biscuits with the butter mixture.

Uncle Roy's
Biscuits

🥄 Prep Time: 20 mins
🕐 Total Time: 50 mins

Servings per Recipe: 12
Calories   157 kcal
Fat   8.3 g
Carbohydrates   17.8g
Protein   2.9 g
Cholesterol   22 mg
Sodium   196 mg

Ingredients

2 C. all-purpose flour
1 tbsp baking powder
1 tsp salt
1 tbsp white sugar
1/3 C. shortening
1 C. milk

Directions

1. Set your oven to 400 degrees F before doing anything else.
2. In a large bowl, mix together the flour, baking powder, sugar and salt.
3. With a pastry cutter, cut the shortening and mix till a coarse meal forms.
4. Slowly, add the milk and mix till the dough pulls away from the side of the bowl.
5. Place the dough onto a floured surface, and knead for about 15-20 times.
6. Roll the dough to 1-inch thickness and with a large cutter, cut the biscuits.
7. Arrange the biscuits onto an ungreased baking sheet and cook in the oven for about 13-15 minutes.

HOMEMADE
Doggie Biscuits

Prep Time: 30 mins
Total Time: 45 mins

Servings per Recipe: 4
Calories	465 kcal
Fat	24.5 g
Carbohydrates	53.1g
Protein	8.2 g
Cholesterol	65 mg
Sodium	834 mg

Ingredients

1 C. cornmeal
2 C. all-purpose flour
1 tsp salt
1 egg
3 tbsp vegetable oil
1/2 C. chicken broth

2 tsp chopped fresh parsley

Directions

1. Set your oven to 400 degrees F before doing anything else and grease a cookie sheet.
2. In a large bowl, mix together the flour, cornmeal and salt.
3. In another bowl, add the egg and oil and beat well.
4. Stir in the chicken broth and parsley.
5. Slowly, add the egg mixture into the flour mixture mixing till a soft dough forms.
6. Place the dough onto a lightly floured surface and knead it lightly.
7. Roll the dough to a 1/2-inch thickness and with the cookie cutters, cut into desired shapes.
8. Place cookies onto prepared cookie sheet in a single layer about 1-inch apart and cook in the oven for about 15 minutes.

Weeknight
Biscuit Casserole

Prep Time: 30 mins

Total Time: 1 hr 10 mins

Servings per Recipe: 6

Calories	450 kcal
Fat	13.2 g
Carbohydrates	48g
Protein	33.5 g
Cholesterol	96 mg
Sodium	2015 mg

Ingredients

1/4 C. butter
2 cloves garlic, minced
1/2 C. chopped onion
1/2 C. chopped celery
1/2 C. chopped baby carrots
1/2 C. all-purpose flour
2 tsp white sugar
1 tsp salt
1 tsp dried basil

1/2 tsp ground black pepper
4 C. chicken broth
1 (10 oz.) can peas, drained
4 C. diced, cooked chicken meat
2 C. buttermilk baking mix
2 tsp dried basil
2/3 C. milk

Directions

1. Set your oven to 325 degrees F before doing anything else and grease a 13x9-inch baking dish.
2. In a large skillet, melt the butter on medium-high heat and sauté the celery, onion, carrots and garlic till tender.
3. Stir in the flour, sugar, dried basil, salt and black pepper.
4. Add broth and bring to a boil, stirring continuously.
5. Boil for about 1 minute and stir in the peas.
6. Simmer for about 5 minutes and stir in the chicken.
7. Place the chicken into prepared baking dish.
8. In a medium bowl, mix together the baking mix and 2 tsp of the dried basil.
9. Add milk and mix till a dough forms.
10. Divide the dough into 6-8 balls.
11. Place the dough onto floured wax paper and with the palm of your hand, flatten each ball of dough into a circular shape.
12. Place the balls on the top of chicken mixture.
13. Cook in the oven for about 30 minutes.
14. Cover with a foil paper and cook in the oven for about 10 minutes further.
15. While serving, place the chicken mixture over biscuits.

BEEF
Biscuits

Prep Time: 20 mins
Total Time: 45 mins

Servings per Recipe: 10

Calories	306 kcal
Fat	18.9 g
Carbohydrates	15.5g
Protein	18.4 g
Cholesterol	76 mg
Sodium	632 mg

Ingredients

1 1/4 lb. lean ground beef
1/2 C. chopped onion
1/4 C. chopped green chili pepper
1 (8 oz.) can tomato sauce
2 tsp chili powder
1/2 tsp garlic salt

1 (10 oz.) can refrigerated buttermilk biscuit dough
1 1/2 C. shredded Monterey Jack cheese, divided
1/2 C. sour cream
1 egg, lightly beaten

Directions

1. Set your oven to 375 degrees F before doing anything else.
2. Heat a large skillet and cook the beef, green chili pepper and onion till browned completely.
3. Drain the excess grease from the skillet.
4. Stir in the tomato sauce, chili powder and garlic salt and simmer while preparing the biscuits.
5. Separate the biscuit dough into 10 biscuits and pull each biscuit into 2 layers.
6. Place the 10 biscuit halves on the bottom of a 9-inch pie dish and press to form the bottom crust.
7. Reserve the other 10 biscuit halves for the top layer.
8. Remove the beef mixture from the heat and stir in 1/2 C. of the cheese, sour cream, and egg.
9. Place the mixture over bottom crust and top with the remaining biscuit halves to form the top crust.
10. Sprinkle with the remaining cheese evenly.
11. Cook in oven for about 25-30 minutes.

Wifey's
Favorite

Prep Time: 20 mins
Total Time: 25 mins

Servings per Recipe: 12

Calories	173 kcal
Fat	9.4 g
Carbohydrates	19.1g
Protein	3.1 g
Cholesterol	17 mg
Sodium	271 mg

Ingredients

2 C. all-purpose flour
2 tbsp white sugar
4 tsp baking powder
1/2 tsp cream of tartar
1/2 tsp salt
1/2 C. vegetable shortening
1 egg

2/3 C. milk

Directions

1. Set your oven to 450 degrees F before doing anything else.
2. In a bowl, sift together the flour, baking powder, sugar, cream of tartar, and salt.
3. With a pastry cutter, cut the shortening and mix till a coarse crumb forms.
4. In another bowl, add the milk and egg and beat well.
5. Slowly, add the milk mixture in the flour mixture, mixing till well combined.
6. With a spoon, place the mixture onto a cookie sheet and cook in the oven for about 10 - 12 minutes.

Printed in Great Britain
by Amazon